MORE FLOWERS

More Flowers
by Susan L. Leary

Copyright © Feburary 01, 2026 Susan L. Leary

No part of this book may be used or performed without written consent of the author, if living, except for critical articles or reviews.

Leary, Susan L.
1st edition

ISBN: 978-1-949487-52-7
Library of Congress Control Number: 2025943055

Interior design by Natasha Kane
Cover design by Joel W. Coggins
Cover art by Yuliya Derbisheva / iStockPhoto
Editing by Kris Bigalk

Copyright © 1994 by Ursula K. Le Guin
First appeared in GOING OUT WITH PEACOCKS AND OTHER POEMS, published by Harper Perennial in 1994. Reprinted by permission of Ginger Clark Literary, LLC

THE LETTERS OF EMILY DICKINSON, edited by Cristanne Miller and Domhnall Mitchell, Cambridge, Mass.: The Belknap Press of Harvard University Press, Copyright © 2024 by the President and Fellows of Harvard College. Copyright © 1958 by the President and Fellows of Harvard College. Copyright © renewed 1986 by the President and Fellows of Harvard College. Copyright © 1914, 1924, 1932, 1942 by Martha Dickinson Bianchi. Copyright © 1952 by Alfred Leete Hampson. Copyright © 1960 by Mary L. Hampson. Used by permission. All rights reserved.

Trio House Press, Inc.
Minneapolis
www.triohousepress.org

for my mother

Table of Contents

Pseudo Myth   3

We Examined Survival under a Microscope   7
Photograph Theory   8
Uprooted   9
There Are No Warning Signs   10
The Fifth Swan   11
Ox Walking on Ice   12
Snow, Almost, Nearly   13
Some Other Girl   14
At First, Obedience, Subsequently—   15
Self-Portrait with Fiction & Oversized Eye   16
Strawberry Season   17
Encore to Girlmaking   18
Brief History of Light   19

Subject(ivity)   23
The Language of Women   24
When a Man Cries, We Make Light of Our Own Laughter   25
The World Ends When We Do   26
Government   27
Knitted Wings   28
Maternal Caress, 1896   29
We Create a Belief System from the Ruins   30
Inheritances of a Twilighted Hour   31
God Makes Every Woman a Widow   32
Feast   33
Telephone, Ad Infinitum   34
A Bird Named Ego, or Head Exploding with a Woman   35

Now That My Mother Has Apologized	36
Girl House with Epigenetic Effect, or, A Tumult of Flowers	37
The 89th Constellation	38
We Write the Sad Things, or We Write What Happened	39

Entertainer of the Year	43
Still Life with Rendezvous & Presumption	45
Dramatic Irony	46
Existential Poem on a Monday	48
Poem in which God or I Go Missing	49
A Student Says 'Empathy Doesn't Make Sense'	50
Neither David nor Goliath	51
Contemplating the Wrong Miracles	52
Everything Is Different When the Weather Is Different	53
Alibi	54
The Kids These Days Want to Be Happy	55
A Room for Future Recognition	56
Self-Portrait as Loose Change	57
Daytime Manifesto	59
Holding My Skeleton to the Light	60
I Don't Want to Write about Flowers	61

In Lieu of Flowers, More Flowers	65
Heirloom, Atmosphere, Lilies	66
River Bride	67
Idle	68
On Sundays, I Do Laundry	69
Before, the Usual Months—	70
The Color of Wheat	71
I, the Unruliest Flower, Buried Winter	72
Brief History of Systems	73
The Feather Hour	74
Because My Tongue Is Not Welcome Here	75

Notes	77
Acknowledgments	79
Gratitude	83
About the Author	85

I am out with lanterns, looking for myself.

—Emily Dickinson

The offering of flowers / is a work of generations.

—Ursula K. Le Guin

Pseudo Myth

Again, I've confused   the horseman for the horse,
the artillery of a muscle   for a minor hero's sling.
What we do in the name   of obedience, not
thinking wonder has   anything to gain over wit.
The wheel, at times,   will envy the hands that
clutch it. The horse,   the inoperable reigns. Trust
me. I, who have neither   head nor heart, whose
name is not mine but Girl.   What's torn through
the center is as good a guide   as any.

We Examined Survival under a Microscope

Held a ten-second funeral for the fly, then for its frayed
wing, watched as a familiar garden loosed lavender hymns
into the 'thinking part' of the brain. Tulips, the first to empty

themselves of a body—the only sound: a pair of knees
knocking in the airstream. I was a shy child, which is to say
death is the supreme invention. Not medicine, not laser

focus, rather the knot of weeds that overtook my hands
as I dragged my skull into the schoolyard. All cruelties traipse
inward. As light thaws into a river, not even the river

will acquire the skills to notice me. Everything is a labor.
Joy. Courtesy. The dying dog sunning in the grass, the attention
it troubles me to give her. As if by habit, dusk does not exceed

a single hour. Carefully, I dress in another girl's arms & legs,
wear her checkered uniform to bed. The dark before me, that deep
nothing, how even nothing seemed to possess a face.

Photograph Theory

I grew up next to a power plant in the Midwest
& whenever a friend came over, I asked my mother
to take her home. Earnestness can be unbearable:
the girl who pulled the plastic horse's mane straight
from its scalp, then tried her lips at my harmonica.

There should be a blood test for the emotions,
simple instructions folded onto a slip of paper & slid
inside a test tube. Sometimes, the illness is the consolation.
Sometimes, amid nuclear war, not even your mother
can hold the catmint in full bloom.

How often is language the arbitrary injury & not
the lack thereof? At the meal table: *What's been going on
at school, dear? Have you been giving your teachers
any trouble?* The only recourse: to collapse into doggedness
as much as self-pity, try my hand at the piano again.

But the nervous system is a wreck & those hands worn
clean with Palmolive. Self-talk, hardly useful. Improve
your stamina, girl. Dab the corners of your mouth with a rider's
handkerchief or risk the embarrassment of eating. My god.
The times I've heard life is looking happily into a camera. I say,

                        even when photographed I do not exist.

Uprooted

Not circumstance or whim, but
discipline, is what it took. My legs
were skinned raw & my face
throbbed of collateral damage.
The word 'vulgar' became
synonymous with disuse, with five tons
of scrap metal along the roadside
& wildflowers flattened
into bone-dust. My own shame
felt pleasing: all those stammerings
around the eye, the deer standing
there dumbstruck. How does
a *self* happen when of what we bury
& what we unearth, there's no
telling the difference? Sometimes,
the cold's brute stamina is so
terribly miserable, I almost forget
I was a child. That the dried leaves
were taught to ridicule us & yet
how unexpectedly: the heart.
So much persuasion inside
the body of a dead thing. What,
of any of this, is holy? The geese fly
south while we commit to a false
& unflagging attention. This
is precise as I can be. There were cars
everywhere but no people. People
everywhere but no sound.

There Are No Warning Signs

Yet there's the invasive smell of sliced oranges—the obstinate
mother: the soft body that falls hard to sleep in a stranger's
mouth. Red light travels the most miles through the atmosphere
& bitter to no end, we become the red tape we rue. All of us,
the unnavigable road forward. Despite the wildness of our tongues,
the rumor wants nothing for itself but silence. The hour that's passed,
an honest farewell. When did the holiness of the day
communicate a desire to be worshipped, the red
geraniums a desire to signal a home? Somehow, we've
become the fool yet spared ourselves the reddening face.
Let a better version of accomplishment begin here: with the violent
hand that sets down the non-violent whip. With the untilled
acre. The red dress hanging in the back of the closet
waiting to be worn. There's no way around it: if we are to speak
of ourselves, we must speak of what
we've wounded.

The Fifth Swan

Is the image that provided a set of subsequent images
for me to avoid: rain collected in a metal pail. Birdsong at
midnight. I say I am no different. I left my girlhood
bleeding at the back door & ignored her letters. Promised
to replicate her as image, then made her sound.
Listen—anywhere you look, the highway is fifty yards
away, which means we are abandoned
by the present as fast as we are abandoned by myth:
despite snow, the sun throbs & the lakes devour themselves
whole. Thinking myself smart, I google images
of bedrooms erected in the forest & capitalize
only the important words to make them real. I left my Girlhood
bleeding at the back door & ignored her letters. Girlhood,
Girl, Rendezvous, Sleep. Recall, it was furniture
in the old days that was made well. My heart, a piece
of furniture with loose threads & a broken leg,
so I whittle a table & chair from neither image nor sound
but the mind—& if through the mind, the concept
of death can be reinvented, the fifth swan
is no longer dead, the lake is teeming & snow
glues itself to the ground: the back door swung open. The only
question, who is more distrusting: you or the world?
The rain or the pail. The birds or the sky. For the sake of the swans,
I give up, though the soul must sit down to make amends.

Ox Walking on Ice

I should say
defeat has made me
capable. Instead, it has terrified me
of endings & despite my efforts, the house
is going to pot. Most nights, my mother spends
drafting a set of instructions: *Outside, do the work yourself*
until it is physically impossible. If it's a limb, cut on an angle. Cypress
mulch will deter any ants. Surprise me with a white rose bush
near Mary. As obedient as I am I can mythologize
anybody's death but I cannot mythologize
my mother's. Still, I continue to be
impressed by the willfulness
of living things. The voice
box buried inside
a stretch of meadow. The ox
walking on ice. Even in war, the last
hour is for loving, when every girl wears
the rain like a philosophy or a dress. As now,
an anonymous wound rouses in her little cot, healed
& disturbed, finding it difficult to adore the sun. It's me,
stranded at the shoreline in my best dress, pink
& gauzy, waiting for rescue. The weather,
a useful disguise. Remember
me. I don't want
that ship to
come.

Snow, Almost, Nearly

There's a certain surrender
to being an optimist—one which begins
with the day but, in fact, begins

with the evening. With dusk
crocheted into winter & a girl's dress
hanging by the hem of nightfall.

We find things most beautiful
in the act of their dying. Bright
red leaves. A refusal to eat. The child

who goes to school & the mother
who drives back from school
alone. Yet here, the birds are so lurid

against an opalness of sky. The rain,
serener than we'd ever imagined. Someone,
always, to speak with ease & someone

to cover the eyes. Let me contemplate
my own role in this, or let me burrow within a frailty
of prayer. The cold, an interminable elegy.

There's nothing left to forgive. Twice,
I was long ago buried. I discover
this thing called snow.

Some Other Girl

Has been
asked to watch
my belongings.
She is every
substitute
for handsome.
Girlhood, subject
to assemblage.
When I return,
two sets
of nightclothes
are laid out
on a bench.
Snow rippling
across a pair
of scissors.
In class, the girl
& I learn
the world
inside the world
is flourishing.
A girl suffers.
Form suffers.

At First, Obedience, Subsequently—

Defiance. The wound,
        begging for attention: its half heart
beating beneath a lace doily while the ugliness

        explodes to the surface. Why
disrupt this flourish of peace, this little tomb of
        white space? *She looks good*,

they'd said. Brave inside unworkable
        conditions. Dead or alive, we make an
anniversary of our sorrow, expeditious

        with our buckets of spring. To what do we owe
the pleasure? You fabricate worlds
        in dreams while a girl fabricates worlds

on the page. *This* is what is meant by ritual.
        When we say, the pedigree of the mouth-
body is good. There's no use determining for whom

        our company is intended. Every gesture
is dangerous. Were I to cut my ear off,
        I'd give it to you.

Self-Portrait with Fiction & Oversized Eye

All fiction begins with the exposure of a nest. In winter:
tin rain. The grass vanished. A medieval take on sky
& earth. To say childhood is trending is not preposterous
in the least. I lived here & in a single day, I grew up.

A tumbling of saplings, then a tumbling of hierarchies—
every tree but one erased. Beneath the gaunt limbs, an aristocrat
in a velvety cloak examining the earth with his thoroughly
oversized eye. & because all fiction is action, I count

the bones alongside him. I count every frayed wing
placed inside a bowl that is really my skull made of twigs.
Remnant as remnant as proof of healing as false proof
of sky. Again, I begin in a room I cannot touch. One that is image

husked of all drama. & do you believe me? The faint prickling
inside my hand, when opened: pollen, spring …

Strawberry Season

The concept of *again* is tragic, humility as undervalued
as the accurate perception of a woman's terror. Again, I am owed
a meal, but when winter arrives in the shape of an apology, I cease
to forage my bones. A dog barks in the apartment

below me & the phone rings promptly at noon. What a mother
knows is very random & very particular at once. It's strawberry season.
What we can & cannot pray for. Which cardigan. To wash
the blood out with cold water. When fate stops her weeping,

it's all uphill from there. On the desk, the sun's heart exploding inside
the torso of an iris. Across the forest floor, a rabbit's bursting into dust
& echo. There's something to be said for those who say no to beauty,
who provide the flowers their own muses. Thank god for my mother,

her minor invention of language. Only a man's truth shudders
at the feet of lions. Not all animals go somewhere to die.

Encore to Girlmaking

We'll neither hear it nor see it. A girl stepping in
& out of her wound costume, the whole world, a bright
blue hand covering a bright blue mouth. For some, the damage
is plentiful. For some, the luck. Regardless, at daybreak
the fields will undress & step quietly inside
a smaller sea of the hand's body. Anything given
a name is an imitation. Cassiopeia. Orion. The Atlantic.
How so much happens with our backs to the grass.
How even the most stifled lesions have teeth. Interruptions
thrive these days, though I come with my hands wrapped dotingly
around the hollowness of affect. Daily, the horizon engages
in concessions with the evening & most animals seen
roaming the fields are companionless. We, too, are justly
purposeful as we rake the heavier debris from the sky. The stars
witness everything—as does the mouth—& as a girl reenters
the scene, it will surprise you, though not in the least, that the stars
are the most compassionate of all.

Brief History of Light

Too often, I am planning for the unkindness of structures:
adjectives, Monday morning's committee meeting, loose floorboards
in the attic, coffee that misses the cup. If I am monstrous
it is because others tell me I am monstrous. I hone my skills. I sharpen
the blade. I make my enemies the most unforgettable
cup of tea. Still, the man I share an office with tells me I have
a small footprint, as if it were something to be
proud of. What I could get away with, I think, with such
tininess, chewing a handful of flowers, then blooming a field
of mice from my throat. I could be so microscopic no one would see
me running across their graves nor hear my whisper, urging people back
into their clothes. I am so accustomed to being
counted out, I don't even know what it is
to be lonely. & what a privilege to want to be lonely.
But in my dreams, I am a kid again & my mother is at the counter
mixing batter into a bowl. She is every shade of yellow: yellow
hair, yellow smile, yellow cake. Around her, a hundred suns
strung from the ceiling. When I tell her I am tired of being the hidden
door others walk through to arrive at an epiphanic
moment, she explains the most entertaining TV shows
are those with two characters & zero plot. That is, no structure,
no playbook, no dessert. & that the sun is sunless—that in no way
can it ever ascertain itself—does this make the sun a room
or a door? A question I never ask the woman who always finds a way
to behold me. & even now, as I walk hand-in-hand
with my adult shadow around an impressively man-made
lake, I survive not because I am an expert in jousting but because I am
loved. Because my mother was the window & she let me be the light.

Subject(ivity)

Between a mother
& child passes
information that otherwise
could not exist.
That no one else
can know.
The mother, the healer
& the wound
maker. The child,
the mother's biographer.

The Language of Women

Before I am blood, heartbeat, or bone, I begin as language. As rude message snaked through a mezzanine of sky. A man speaks for no reason other than his own & the words lodge themselves inside the stray womb of a woman. This is no miracle. My mother, your mother can be any sheep from the flock. A wolf howls & Mary is the chosen one. A wolf howls & in the back of a woman's mind, not even Mary can avoid the advances of God. & so every woman is a girl. Young girl. Servant girl. A girl who knows what lives inside a man's mouth can be more barbarous than sex. Because it is the girl who must now explain herself. *Pregnant. Accident. Because what else could I do?* Young girl, she could be my sister ovaling the sweep of me in her arms. Young girl, she tells the story of a different wolf. Girl wolf. Mother wolf. A wolf that out of love or destruction once fed upon an entire forest, the froth of tulips dusting her snout & moss lining her belly. That there be nothing more to scavenge. No women & no sheep. All around her, fresh blood. Men, in their desperation, fallen to the knees having cut their own tongues from their throats. This is the miracle. A girl who refuses to neither hear nor spare the false speech of false gods, snakes her own language through sky. Saying, *Child, you are beautiful. Child, you are mine.*

When a Man Cries, We Make Light of Our Own Laughter

Because it takes a woman more time than a man
to feel sentimental. For a man, every story, a war story.
Every story, an occasion for flowers. There are histories
of rivers & there are histories of men who cross them.
Men who feast upon the dramatic snow-swell of winter,
of even the ice. In the movies, it is always the woman
who watches the man watch *his* life flash before his eyes.

A man emerges profound & a woman beams at the discovery,
as if it were profound to love one's family, as if a father
did not know in the other room, he could hear his children
singing. In the kitchen, a woman tends to flowers
& spoons soup, her hands perpetually smelling of metal.
She is beautiful because she is stoic, flooding history
with lessons that do not mistake country for kin.

When a man cries, this woman will draw his hand into hers
& caress his cheek, a gesture for which she is considered
strong. There is irony here, a hidden message. Look closer.

The World Ends When We Do

Because a bullet entering the body is not a matter
of machinery but of an ache in the fields. Because a man
commanded a woman to hand-stitch the uniforms
& papier-mâché the wounds. Because there is trauma
in the tenderness. Who wants to be an understudy
when the performance cares little for its actors? The whale
swallows Jonah whole & a man convinces himself a lost
limb means *keep fighting*, while women bandage the blood-soaked
sky with soiled rags & serve an invisible God crumb cake
on a platter. What we offer each other is worse
than what is withheld. Symbolism. Something to drink.
The promise of land. No, darling. We must hold
our breath & drain the face of its color. Punctuate the image
with fact: in war portraits, it is always the woman
holding the gun.

Government

A god spends the evening rearranging
the siblings in their beds. Each child is a misbehaved
angel, each limb demanding the attention of a heart
by skirting the immortal hand. It takes an honest bystander
to draw back the leaves & account for the knot
inside the sister & the name inside the brother. The knot,
which grows deep among her eye sockets, heavy
with rain. The name, which burrows into the dried
earth of the sister's stomach, an ephemeral fire
of winter that disrobes the trees of their sorrows & offers
last season's nest. So much to be seen—& we hope
to be seen in sleep more than we hope we may
never die. Such little time for redundancy. & because
there are two mouths, the children never run out
of things to say, even while tumbling & tumbling against
the immortal hands, the sounds of their togetherness
caught inside a paper bag. The mouth, a hand; a hand,
a mouth; the mouth covering a hand. Why resolve
this tension? Even in spring, the flowers were so crestfallen
& hibernating. Even in spring & asked what happened,
the children never named what they saw.

Knitted Wings

Quiet in its jawing,
winter settles upon
the earth. The gunshot
becomes the brushstroke
& the birds, lightly grazed, are
broken. Dead leaves peek
through snow like cut crusts of
bread.
Like tiny sutures, like
bird beaks. Winter, a violence   Or
that softens   not.
into its prey as a hand brought
tenderly to the forehead by
a mother. Winter, the sudden
blow. Winter, aspirin
on the counter, the
birds bandaged & restored to
the sky.

Everything that happens
in winter happens by
candlelight. We see the
burgeoning shadows,
the inelegant structures, the bones
& not the meat. The way we
know the sorrow of an animal
without any sign
of a whimper, limp, or blood.
The way even the best mothers
can fuck a child up. Prepare
for her bird only knitted
wings. As in another season
when the snow stops & the rain
stops & the sky remembers
its drought, in an open field, water
sometimes helps
fire along.

Maternal Caress, 1896

after Mary Cassatt

Before my mother was my mother, she was a painting
in a textbook, an image I study of a mother & daughter crouched
in a meadow & facing one another, the mother
clutching the girl's arm & the girl clutching her mother's
cheek. There is the theme of domesticity. Of intimacy.
There are the expressive brushstrokes. An expansiveness of green.
Somedays, I want to study my mother. I want to clutch
her face & hold the smallest version of her in my eye. That she can be made
strange to me is what most makes her my mother. & inside that
strangeness, or tenderness, the tall grass would forget it was a meadow
& the green of the entire world would be drowned.

We Create a Belief System from the Ruins

I understand the world through the process
of elimination: eradicate the tent, eradicate the sleeping
& what remains are the children. Except in the fable
of my personhood, the backyard is an inefficient
wood & dusk crawls out of a hole. Was I aware the light
was an undertaker, that the uninfringeable gray
could be this gray? Every question is another reframing
of the problem. I am the daughter of a girl, sitting
upright at the eternal desk of my mind, sorting
a tenement of numbers & colors, arms crushed beneath
the body. The work, as is all work, is unglamorous,
which is why they call it *work*, which is why the imagination
is a kind of (dis)order. & what if I died like this? The sun,
a miniscule star in the early life of a routine, angels
playing piano at some other girl's feet, the flat grass sprung
into shadow. I say now there are no ruins, that against the heft
of grammar, girlhood is no corrective measure. The world
returns: I make a bed of myself. I sleep inside it.

The world returns: I make a bed of myself. I sleep
inside it. I say now there are no ruins, that against the heft
of grammar, girlhood is no corrective measure. The sun,
a miniscule star in the early life of a routine, angels
playing piano at some other girl's feet, the flat grass sprung
into shadow. The work, as is all work, is unglamorous,
which is why they call it *work*, which is why
the imagination is a kind of (dis)order. & what if
I died like this? I am the daughter of a girl, sitting upright
at the eternal desk of my mind, sorting a tenement
of numbers & colors, arms crushed beneath
the body. Every question is another reframing
of the problem. Was I aware the light was an undertaker,
that the uninfringeable gray could be this gray?
I understand the world through the process of elimination:
eradicate the tent, eradicate the sleeping & what remains
are the children. Except in the fable of my personhood,
the backyard is an inefficient wood & dusk crawls out of a hole.

Inheritances of a Twilighted Hour

I ask the realtor if the previous owner died inside & she repeats
the kitchen is updated, that from the window above the sink,

there's a view of an imaginary lake that mimes the color play
in the backsplash. To think the grass has disappeared

to the banyan trees in a longing for sun. Rather, the green ardors
razed by a trek of boys armed into men, a glut of roots tramping

sludge through the house as they invade the firmament. It's safe
to say the locks will need changing. That, as in the movies,

by tomorrow, a mother will be devising cheap dresses
from the drapes. The day after, yet another erecting a heart-shaped

house beneath a canopy of clean sheets where any daughter
can roam. Soon, expectation returned to the mouths of girls once

sunk in the mere, their faces knocking at the shallows
in want of an old verse netted by the cupboards. Somewhere,

troops are gaining ground & a restless soldier is begging, skillfully,
for a meal, bullets disguising themselves in the air as chimes. The wind,

bitter with rain. Why the realtor says I should fear the living more
than the dead. Why my mother says, *Come girl, give me a hand.*

God Makes Every Woman a Widow

An early lesson—myself, five-years-old & my grandmother explaining the importance of a triangle. The folded red, white, & blue handed to her at my granddaddy's funeral by a soldier. A man, among other men, who had fired a gun into the sky. What happens to a bullet that enters the earth aimed at nothing? It becomes a small pillow, the perfect size for a resting head—& my grandmother lets me rest, the afternoon light angling into her bedroom grazing my legs just below the knees. With my head among the taut stars, I think about triangles, about the precise relationship between a war, a woman, & peace. I think of faith, which my grandmother wants more of these days, explaining how so much of love is believing ideas about the world that aren't true. Mostly, that loss is fashioned into a three-point shape so God can prove his hands are clean.

Feast

In Slovene, the month of February translates to the month
of cutting down trees. Also, the month of women tying a goat
to every stump. Because goats are tree-eaters & very useful
should a dying thing momentarily be tempted by life.

Half the world's trees are said to be felled for reasons tied
to human survival. Naturally, we fail to see the ways in which
the goats are far braver than us, unflinching in their position
to gnaw & glut on another thing clinging to endure—what God

has done to women for centuries. From every stump, God's
forgotten breath advancing through the outermost layers of stem
& root, through the tiniest shoots of green. More reason to believe
February the most intuitive & counterproductive month.

Because it takes seven to eight trees, or rather, an epic
of goats & women to produce enough oxygen for one person
to breathe an entire year. So tell me: how many devastations
before spring will it take to sustain us all?

Telephone, Ad Infinitum

A daughter tells her mother the same story for one hundred years &
the mother never tires of it. In the story, two female birds exchange
wings & beaks & then exchange songs—   but the mechanism
of exchange is never clear because there were never any birds
to begin with. Only the idea of two birds with no apparent
purpose other than to make a miracle of time. This is
the origin of inheritance, which is also the origin
of personality, which might be the origin
of love. The undeniable sturdiness
of a spectacular set of bones &
feathers each afternoon asleep
in the grass, waiting
to reassemble.

A Bird Named Ego, or Head Exploding with a Woman

The gods may thieve fire & wield the hammer & nails
but within the chests of men, women conceal a bird
with clipped wings & name each bird Ego. The bird loves
itself more than it loves the man & must rely, reluctantly,
on the false asset of a body to provide the soundest
fibers for its nest. The men expect no different
& contend with a fervor until the bird apprehends
its purpose, the untrimmed beaks scraping against the hearts'
walls like an inexperienced angel fumbling the scissors
that severed her from the earth. Who was it that first
determined the responsibilities of the gods? Rhea bore
Zeus in secret & Zeus's greatest deed? His head
exploding with a woman who convinced the masses
no bird were tyrannical, that neither could a bird
be possessed. Under certain circumstances, a clipped wing
may even save a wild creature's life, restrain the bird's
urge to scale the highest pitch when sensing fury
or betrayal. & as you charge forth flaunting a sword meant only
to keep you busy, know from within a transplanted little
womb, a bird is singing. Botched gods, bedecked in the mail
of your brawn, you are precisely the men we made you.

Now That My Mother Has Apologized

In the bathroom mirror, the soft configuration of her face. Toweling off my hair or brushing my teeth, it knows to startle, offering itself nightly in the surest flashes through mine. Eye through eye, light through light, is this mercy or a muddle of stars? A flicker of my girl-life's apocalypse. I want to say I don't care what my mother thinks of me now nor ever, but how could this be true when our mothers are the only real gods? Even now at the sink, she resists my every attempt to steady her, yet there she is looking back at me, warped to impossible perfection like one of Dali's ticking clocks. What is it I have been waiting for from this part ghost of a woman who insists on tangling the threads? Until, in turning from the mirror, I see my mother, seeing me as I have so badly wanted to be seen.

Girl House with Epigenetic Effect, or, A Tumult of Flowers

Through a lit window in the soil, an unseen
garden. Ear to the ground & a whimper
        of blood.   The unholy histories of a thousand
                dresses   suddenly   clamoring against skull
& bone, clamoring with the heft of roses against
the eaves.   Girl, you bloom just the same, perpetually engaged
        in a long argument, blade
                held scrupulously
                      to the neck. Nothing lets up because the blade
is you, is your mother, is the scent of marigolds
        balled into a fist.   Is—   every rain-swelled seed sunned
into shadow before another man makes the whole world
creak.   Upstairs, yours too a humble
        mouth, a tiny ache   burst   into a tumult
                                  of flowers.

The 89th Constellation

It is rumored that when we speak,
        we speak the language of God—

a strange divinity of twig & berry
        loosed from the citadels of our tongues …

their bodies—   now *birds*,
        constellated in the firmament.

Oh, how we animate inside the translucence
        of every eye.

We must be lovely indeed.

We Write the Sad Things, or We Write What Happened

What happened was my mother couldn't leave me
So wherever I looked there was a face. There was an ear
& a mouth. Ice wrapped in a towel & a hand wrapped around
My smaller one. For purple day, the purple shirt washed
& ironed. Early evenings & a warm meal, another
Practice, details that somehow feel like any other day
Yet accumulate into the entirety of a life. 30 years later
& I'm childless. Maybe because I want to be. Maybe because
In the next room, people are talking & I'm supposed to be good
With my words. Meanwhile, I wake alone each morning
In polished clothes & deliver on a life in fear of the kindest words
Anyone could say of me: *That woman? She's just a mother.*

Entertainer of the Year

Before the lilac bushes were cut down,
there were mornings the purplish
stems wrapped in tin foil could bring
a person happiness. Schoolchildren
made the nuns happy with their bouquets
& the mothers were happy to hear it.
I was once that giddy. I believed
in drinks with a lover, the work
of my hands, the afterlife. Wallace Stevens
says God & the imagination are one,
but the nuns of my mother's childhood
chose the convent because it was easy
to walk away & retain your dignity.
Now, the world is replete with people
who'll have you practice gratitude
& affix your daily affirmations
to the mirror. Like any good therapist,
I prefer cause & effect to *everything happens
for a reason*. I prefer harboring a fugitive
to the centuries-long controversy
between the sky & the stars. We can't fight
the inevitability of our disasters,
but we can be Entertainer of the Year.
The only form of critique, to cut
the shape of ourselves from immediate
chaos & bury it inside our mouths.
Don't be a stranger, they say,
but when someone implies I have
the key to survival, they haven't caught on
to the fact that of self-awareness,
there can be too much of a good thing.
Like magnets on the fridge,
smart is the new sexy; the loudest
bird, the quietest bird; the protagonist,
the self-deluding villain. What it says
of humanity that pretending is the last
act of our volition? Just yesterday
on the phone, I ask my mother

about the children & she recalls the budding
warmth outside, the fresh scent
of lilacs, her mother wrapping the stems
as if the limbs of angels. How easy
it was to believe her. How easy.
The flowers made the children that happy.

Still Life with Rendezvous & Presumption

We romanticize the separateness of animals
only to spoil the head that lifts itself to us in the magnolia
fields with its chandelier of antlers & silken chestnuts

for judgments. Beauty of this kind can mean almost anything,
certainly that we make ourselves more quietly human, immediately
small & slowish or else risk the mirage that already refuses

our involvement, says no to the outstretched hand. Still,
we presume we can minimize the terror, afford the deer
proper conditions to be among us. In our vigilance, we notice

everything: the patch of dampened blossoms, a faint ear-twitch,
the near invisible insects afloat in the ether's crown. Yet, how deeply
we fail at introspection, supposing the deer were to stumble

upon us in the same field, he'd attend instinctively to our tiring
wildness, that he'd gain considerably much from watching us
with our eyes closed, from watching us be us but asleep.

Dramatic Irony

It's an unfair criticism,
but in the wild, a herd
of impala will cross the river
either too stupidly
or too cooperatively,
as if a slight hesitation
at the water's edge
were adequate to detect
the leathery beasts awaiting
a meal. At home, the scene
unfolds on the TV & we delude
ourselves with the musical
accompaniment. The muddy depths,
a shield for the eyes.
Imagination is cruel, too,
which is to say I know
what it means to be dragged
under by workplace politics
or a shitty boyfriend. By men
who hogtie their children
in the cellar. What becomes of us
when we can't recognize
the metaphor? Estranged relatives
will assemble in a field
of gladiolas around a human-
sized box for no reason
other than tradition.
They'll fumble their words,
even though knowing
those words is what makes them
human. It's morally wrong
to dog-ear the pages
of a borrowed book, harps
a friend. Even worse, to feed
the stray cat combing
the dumpster because her hunger
is what keeps her alive.
We think the right decision

will gain us power
or entry, but due diligence
pinpoints only the crocodile
in our lives, not the TV
viewers. The phone charging
by the bedside suggests
I'm a domesticated
animal, yet somewhere
a middle-aged man is laughing
in his pajamas on the couch
& sucking on maraschino
cherries, while I type
the right words
into my Notes App & pretend
I'm not broke or broken-
hearted. In times like these,
choose wisely. In times
like these, it's me
crossing the river. It's me
not knowing I'm dead.

Existential Poem on a Monday

People die all the time on a Monday because the science behind it is so elegant. One more thing crossed off the to-do list: brush your teeth, make coffee, catch a glimpse of your own ghost in the kitchen. On time for once & well-dressed too! But wait, is this yours or someone else's philosophy? Because after work & walking to your car, a small child once tugged at the hem of your dress. Told you Monday is the only day nearest & furthest the Sabbath. What a peculiar thing to say, you thought. What a peculiar thing to find a child, happy & abandoned, in a parking lot. Deep down, you wish to be that child. That good omen parachuted like canned soup from the sky. *Good luck with that*, someone says. You weren't very popular in high school, so it's more than likely your death, too, will be a matter of gossip. Friends will send your mother the wrong kind of flowers & spell your name with an extra "e." *But she was so lovely*, they'll say—*so kind*. & your mother will believe them because every death, as every sorrow, is as vague as the color blue. Egyptian blue. Royal blue. Blue as the blue of Franz Marc's horses. But you already knew that. As you knew your own heart will never muster enough strength to keep you company. Which is why driving home, you move slow past the scene of every accident just to see who's dead.

Poem in which God or I Go Missing

To God's funeral we wear a paper gown
with pockets the size of gills. Inside one pocket, the saddest
grimace. Inside the other, a wind so barbaric, it steals
wildflowers from the earth & filters them through a strobe
light across the dance floor. To celebrate God is to celebrate
capitalism, so there must be order if we are to remain
engaged. All of us, the obedient child with anybody's address
pinned to our shirts. Even the dumbest dog cannot tolerate
reality & waits for a pat on the head. Forgive me,
but I'd rather arrive early to breakfast & late to work, pay
all the bills in scratch-offs. *But we can eat cake!* shouts
the surgeon. *We can pen a thousand eulogies & plunge
to bed in language!* Except that a rich man's scalpel
cannot carve the difference between what's in our pockets
& his. Would anyone bat an eye if God went missing?
If his body were lugged from its ivory casket & exchanged
at Walmart for a cheap apparatus that lets us breathe
undersea? I don't know. But had I heard, swears the surgeon's
son, that wind is the dust of martyrs.

A Student Says 'Empathy Doesn't Make Sense'

Even still, sometimes, we must pull back
the curtains on our own bodies, say, here's my sorrow,
let me show it to you. The hand we're dealt demands
a singular kind of rescue. A bombardment of amber.
The well-remembered weather of our youthful

affairs. Sometimes, persuasion can be a safety, too,
as when we fed lush apples to the horses
straight from our palms. Now, rather than lug our untimely
impatience out into the open field, let's agree
to dissolve the deep quiet that baffles the amusement

of children. Because the sun's out & it's snowing.
A stranger is fleeing the alleyway, barefoot & absent
of warm clothes. Invite her in. What hurts the most in us
can be anybody's business. Our own damage,
the cruelest, most obvious balm.

Neither David nor Goliath

The story must start with a little trouble & in this one,
you're not the hero or the giant but the slingshot.

Niftiness is at its peak & you don't need to be human
anymore to be relevant. David & Goliath isn't about the rise

& fall of the underdog but about making yourself hard
to blame & harder to pity. To hell with legend.

The boy arrived at the scene because earlier that day,
he'd abandoned his sheep, just as doves are known

to haphazardly construct their nests, more interested
in pecking the eyes of some bloody head severed

by a star. You've won & now what? Rather than improbable
skill tidying the slate, everything you've grown

accustomed to becomes a rusted coin or blade. Time,
a costume worn to an interminable party made of overlapping

dreams. I could tell you there's a right way to making
it count, but nowadays wisdom is doled out by computers,

which is not unlike being hit in the skull by a rock.
As you get older: do you seek joy or do you seek fame?

Everyone demands your attention. Your mother, the grocer,
the nagging lamb. The pool attendant, shouting *Don't run!*

when he means to say, *Hey, I was your age once too.*

Contemplating the Wrong Miracles

With sidewalk chalk, I draw the outline of a seesaw
against an open doorway. On one hand, I'm living paycheck
to paycheck & on the other, I'm keeping the orchids alive.

Twice, I misread bullet for ballet, twice think in holding
the riverish image between my fingers, a body's forehead,
its belly. When two people share the same birthday

in the same year, we don't consider the two mothers
on the same day, doing the very same thing.
We think of a consummate romance, the life we love

because we will leave it, not the old bones grazing
a new marvel that is the sky. A tiny space
can have a sky—a wicker casket, a womb, the old organ

referred to as the page. Someday, the only person
who can help you die comfortably will die before you
& you'll rush the hallways, refusing that strange

arrangement of words because in your mind
metaphor is a literal thing, yet it points towards a weather
you've yet to encounter. This time, rather than note

a difference, say plainly what's been misplaced in the mouth.
To those words, don't dare allow me to get used to this,
when it's true we can get used to anything.

Everything Is Different When the Weather Is Different

We packed our bags for a reason. Washed each limb
of the Florida stank & imagined, at daybreak, our bodies asleep
among a pile of horses. Except, the whole concept
of timeliness grew bitter. The first snowfall, a myth & is not
every snowfall a myth? Part fiction, part unrequited love: a means
of articulating when we're confused, all we want are for things
to be otherwise? I expected to be busy. I expected a closed
fist not to be the closest thing to my reflection, a competent
woman to be the surprise victor. Instead, I dressed
the dog in a lavender sweater & spring made a graveyard
of us both. When I first met the man with whom I travel
through this life, we lived three floors apart & the dorm smelled
perpetually of gardenia. We collected flower heads inside
paper bags & verified the color of grass. Which means, beauty
is a fiction, too. That whatever we built, inevitably,
would be committed to the flood. How quickly we forget
there is great freedom in being drowned. Blood, much different
from breath. So we swam against the freeze knowing wholeness
meant brokenness. Knowing in the new city, what we wanted
to be rescued had vanished, that alongside intelligence & unnavigable
terrain, people thrive in permanent aftermath. The fact of our choosing
matters considerably more than the outcome of what we choose.

Alibi

I sat at a desk all day & cracked
jokes. Sometimes I got sick
of the music & sometimes I was
more accountable in my dreams
than in real life. While you
were thinking about me, I wasn't
thinking about you. I was
sucking on gin-gins & funding
my retirement. After the best
news, I took the dog for a walk
& made tea. As a child,
my mother says I preferred talking
to the air. I was still talking.

The Kids These Days Want to Be Happy

So I say, *be happy*, though the instinct in me doesn't capture what I mean. I'd like to think I'd refuse an apology that stumbles drunk out of the bar, that I'd behead my enemies before sharing with them any of the light by which I read. The thing about being "the adult" in the room is you learn rather emphatically how you believe yourself to be isn't how you are. Suddenly, you're before a classroom of eighteen-year-olds scrolling on their cellphones who, someday & mostly for money, wish to open you with their scalpels & manage your stocks. Forget the career center & the proper advice. There're only two options. *Tell me about yourself*, as in the Spartan formality of an interview, or, *Tell me about yourself*, as in soon my dead brother will make his way into the conversation. As in, I'll never be entirely comfortable at the beach, as in, I love clichés as much as I love my mother. Where's that thing you call a heart, the muscle that cuts through the mustard as well as it cuts through you? Be that kid, *be happy*.

A Room for Future Recognition

In the term paper I wrote in graduate school,
I named every blackbird Ophelia, who named the water
after her unborn, who named every tragedy
a sonnet. In the margin, a claim I'd never succeed
in the field unless I learned to play follow
the leader. I hear you—& yet in the unusable heart
of rebuttal, only I know what I sound like
& anger sounds a lot like weeping because the door
is a door & not a window this time. The dying
animal looking to be lost becomes the dead swan
asleep in its feathered body. The dying animal
looking to be lost defies the reason of imagination
& is confused by the unusual gathering
of a crowd, clapping at sunset. Like those before us,
we fail to distinguish the exit from the entrance,
so we float closer & closer to the bank, the brain
asked to replace the wind, the grief-stricken
turning their backs to the water & stuffing their mouths
with chrysanthemums. Until there is no speculation.
Until every other feathered thing moves
to the opposite side of the lake, a muted song carrying
into the endless countryside of evening. In every
world not yet recognized as a world, there is a table,
a lamplight & a stool—a painter filing down teeth
& accentuating the eyes, a new name carved into the quiet
estuary of a man-made box. Any woman, enter stage
right: the last task, to sew the mouth shut.

Self-Portrait as Loose Change

I am neither
heads nor tails
nor a quarter
pulled by
a magician
from behind
the ear of
God. Rather,
I am a dulled
& greening
penny shuffled
beneath three
cups. A makeshift
screwdriver.
Two pieces
of silver placed
upon the eyes
of the dead.
Meaning, some
other fool's
rite of passage
worth no more
than ten minutes
of parking
or half the price
of a load of
wash, as much
a hundred
curse words
as the dreamy
contents of
a pig, vanished
to winter
beneath the
cushions—
though come
summer,
when the sun
is reminded

of its stretch
across the
pool, the sum
of me six feet
deep & gleaming.

Daytime Manifesto

It's not even noon & already a bird flew into the back window
& we named the dead bird Charlie. Rarely is death so quiet.

Rarely do we recognize the sadness before it recognizes us.
Still, we map a way forward, misery camouflaging our tendency

towards music, towards the unforgettable era of car rides
with our mothers. Today, I struggle with progress. Behind

the wheel, no bones to spit, no skeleton dangling at the back
of the throat. Only a pitstop at the nearest exit for an orange

soda & chicken nuggets. I'm average because I want to be.
Because I'm told driving behind the slowest car will save me

from the fires up ahead. But not all birds are resurrected
by food & water. Not all light prevents our thinking about loss.

On the radio, every vanished tune blasting from a preferable
hour. Look at me now, with my hair up & my nails done, arriving

late to the pageant still dressed in yesterday's clothes. I never
want this to be easy, making the most of a life I never asked for.

Holding My Skeleton to the Light

It's possible I watched myself fleeing the alleyway,
myself imagining a series of crueler injuries to the original wound.

What does this mean? asks the poet.
It's contextual! replies anyone without a clue.

This can be a way of describing a metaphor
or a way of describing psychology. This can also be helpful

or not. Listen. When I thought you hadn't the desire
to understand me, I hadn't the desire to be heard.

I Don't Want to Write about Flowers

So much has to happen before a thing can bloom
& so much of what happens we never see. A sprawling narrative
that unfolds beneath the earth before there are scissors
or a kitchen table or the human hand. A flower is without history
because we think we know what happens: soil, seed, sun,
water, bloom. & even if laughter is considered, or drowning
or drought, or one seed's envy of another, we forget
what the flowers may have endured before they were flowers.
Everyone sees our suffering & we must survive
to bloom while a flower *runs its course*, a phrase undressed
of meaning & I am exhausted by meaning. I am
exhausted by the beauty inside the sadness: the solitary flower
outside the jail or the crack of daybreak that slips
between the curtain. Beauty reveals the flawed functioning
of everyday matters, but we forget this, too. All that dirty water,
the chipped vase, the apartment's shaded window. Yet, the flowers
are so well-adjusted. Set towards the sun, they seem to be creating
a language to talk to God. Greedy me, I pluck the flowers. I commit
a minor contentedness. I stow the words in my palm.

In Lieu of Flowers, More Flowers

All we can ask of love is it be reasonable. That the widow
keep her grief to herself & acknowledge the consideration
of the staff. Details make us complicit before they make us
kind & they hardly make the speaker less lonely.

In lieu of flowers, more flowers, as they say. Over the years,
too much will be easy to remember, but what we tolerate
will save us from the undertow. Feeding the dog, folding
summer laundry, on the counter: a vase of flower bones

sunk in copper water. We owe the daytime hours a crown,
the mercy of instinct inside of which we can hear
the ocean, the harp strings that anchor either our readiness
or arbitrariness to the world. All this, too, should count

for something. At sundown, the church hymn from childhood
that gratifies the mouth with its hum. The aftertaste
of green tea. Good television. The mischievousness of a child
who's stayed out past dark, before she's been ruined by the hand.

Heirloom, Atmosphere, Lilies

The cemetery seems always a suitable subject, as there, someone is listening & light seems always to be moving. You can't miss it—just past the gazebo, the solitary bat suspended from the chandeliers with the impartiality of an heirloom. I have a bad habit of being skilled in precisely the wrong ways, of existing like a moth in the closet chewing through the arms of a mink coat, of eating alone in the art room. We all want to be a little improbable, a little cold, though inevitably, pity will mistake the stained glass for exit & we'll think ourselves capable of appearing as fresh nectar poured across the sky.

Rather, there's a breathing body & a swath of stone, more than enough time to muster the silence & avoid the rough plagiarism of the day. Is prayer not marginally unethical? Why should we be allowed to ask the dead for anything? My mother says, *keep going*. Says, in the uninterruptedness of time, ambition will never leave me. That the atmosphere will straighten my spine & suddenly, I'll love what I'm built of. We think heaven is an aperture, all of us tumbling like a curious girl in a blue dress down a bluer hole— but then, the rain picks up & the lilies shake. & there it is, your own jaw, breaking open into your softhearted hands.

River Bride

There's a continent inside our bodies
built from the attar of Eve, a small boat in the river
of our veins & a burned-out church at the fourth

fold in the wrist. We must honor the rib that bears
the raw glow of use, the oar propelling us
to an event for which we're improperly dressed—

the flames marrying the cattails at the water's
edge & the moths breaking free at the broken places.
All we're trying to do is forget where we're going.

We desire a fogged mirror. A row of empty
pews, begging our discovery—any metaphor to thwart
the factual aspect of death. The same is true

in the child's game. A mouth's impulse to choose
truth requires a mild push from the dock, a chipped tooth,
yet we load our boats with remnants of our own failed

harvests & admit the fire does more than keep us warm.
The gospels tell me I lived because God once grabbed evening
by the scruff & declared the world his lover—women

fleeing the abbey to inspect the injuries of small children
blooming in the streets, as if God believed wounds were anything
other than a tarnished ring in the pocket. & the women

did this, why? When a girl returned to the aged
river to hold her skeleton to the light, she'd know
something of this world was gentle.

Idle

Despite madness, beauty. Despite common sense, an idyllic
garden, which in time, makes us ignorant once more. We enter
the shine of the path before we enter the path & I've seen
too many people cry.

Here is a shade of opal. Here, the warmth
of a body just struck at the side of the road. It feels
necessary to justify my behaviors, yet I want nothing more
than privacy.

Snow demanded an alibi. The rumors as apologetic
as the knife. Sometimes, all the dog can do is lie down
at the door to sleep.

Because the title speaks as the title does
& dreams are the first real classroom, says I
who rarely dreams.

On Sundays, I Do Laundry

& there she is—a girl, hidden
inside the rhythmic tumult of a river. As the sun
pours into the kitchen, I take inventory
of a life, her cotton dress breaking
into a meticulous shade of yellow. Water
rushes empty of sound & I am
reminded of the woman in that story who stands in the same
place in her apartment for hours, just
staring ahead. Of how she got there, I am not
to be trusted: a nameless girl must remain
nameless, though am I the girl or the one who refuses
to name her? What is to be freely explained
again tumbling past, then briefly
a hand fitting snug inside my head. & what is the head
without the mouth or the heart? Without the corpse
clad anonymously in dirt? A see-through dress
without pockets? There are more details to the scene: a rubied
horse, a pristine scrap of fabric, a knife
bent atop the river. So I speak
to myself about my body. Touch it to know
it is mine, the hidden-ness a hair shy of being treated
unfairly, or so I am told. & this is what I love
about the rotating dark, about a loose
button, about the water weaving into sunset
& then the sunset & then god: a warm body retrieved from
the flowers, a thread unraveling as it is freed.

Before, the Usual Months—

Now, a thread around the finger, leaving
the imprint of a faulty mood. The dilemma, not that I agreed
to face you in sleep but that night plaited her hair & stood

roadside in strange devotion to the image of a man shoveling
snow. By the time the body unlearns its capacity to bruise, what
I gain will have surpassed the old lessons in art. Tonight,

a stranger's ear sliced from the head & strung like a rusted cow
bell from the ether. Surely, a mother will overhear & deliver
the wildflowers I am told will rescue what is wounded

in us all. Listen as she says, think not of the anguish but lick
every side of the broken mirror. As I wake, trust
the well that flatters us once more.

The Color of Wheat

A heart is breaking—& though outside
everything should be the color of orange,
instead it is the color of wheat.

                        The sun just fallen from the sky
                        & a good dog running through the fields
                        towards God.

The seeds of hundred-year-old poppies
suddenly rising from the soil into heat,
while miles off God prepares

                        the most gorgeous perfume from fire.
                        In its flames, the ghost of a good little girl.
                        Her bones more fragile than flowers.

I, the Unruliest Flower, Buried Winter

On a summer evening in my backyard. I buried
a pack of three-legged wolves & a small girl
who resembled no one I knew. Tamed the day's
mistakes one by one, then flung them into the night's
fist like ivories. They say the first breath is experiment,
though find me a girl who forgets *no* is an anagram
of manhood, that the sixth sense is speech. Words
heaved up from the chest & filling the mouth
like rainwater, like a silk-spun gown. A wolf reborn
& pawing at a phantom limb, the wounds tasting more
of sugar than blood. There is always something
peculiar on the underside of the fabric, roses erupting
through the earth with the muscle of language-scented
beasts. The afterlife entertains not what is good
or bad, only what happened & a girl will take a gun
to her head if it meant the girl were loved. Invent a name
for herself she can survive. Remind me, again,
the lesson. That the stars are the night's pierced ears?
Were we to lose our senses, we'd still know awe.

Brief History of Systems

In crisis, I was unclear. Now, given the task of fitting
the pond to the lily, I say humanity is somewhat
of a layer cake. We work backwards, then side-to-side

& when we slice through the center, we find an artificial
sweetness holding us together: a stack of cash or handkerchief
shaken at the window. There's a dessert-ful-ness

to decision-making. On school nights, I lay my words out
on the bed because we can eliminate *love* from our vocabularies,
but we cannot eliminate *like*. Is it more correct to say

we overcomplicate things or that satire has become
our reality? You think you're finessing me, but I'm finessing you
by letting you *think* you're finessing me, so on & so forth.

Were January to collaborate with June, we'd bypass
winter altogether but like global warming, I'm most efficient
when I leave the dry clothes in the dryer or half my ham

sandwich in the lunch sack. By dinnertime, we'll remember
we are the spell. As Ophelia drowned, water adhered to a woman's
body & white flowers were strewn upon her. I'm still wrapping

my head around it. I'm still wrapping my head around
a bakery in Winona, Minnesota, which set the world record
in 2018 with a 260-layered cake. Were I to lay my skull out

on the bed alongside my words, perhaps I'd unravel the earth
of my mind into a silk scarf, ask someone else to fit the ball
to the yarn or the sky to the ladder, warmth to a woman's neck.

Some facts are proven & some facts are facts. Which is to say,
I barely listened in middle school science class, but I too
am a well-patterned system. World, navigate me.

The Feather Hour

At last, paradise or otherwise. At last,
the meanwhile has fled & the clouds are becoming
clouds once more. Before anything happens, I tell
myself to remember it, intention more god-like
than accuracy, as when the birds fell from the mouth
of a mother & a thousand skies grew beards.

You will want to eat the light. You will want
to build a territory around the illness that destroys
the fields of their conquests. On the tombstone
of the earth, it reads: the heart is polemic
& the brain, an exile. A heavy instrument hammered
inside the body to prove the hurt alone might redeem us.

In any good hour, speak. In any good hour, when
someone arrives to you with a feeling, listen.

Because My Tongue Is Not Welcome Here

I fail at innovation. I am not me
but the animal inside me: a mosquito
cased in amber, the girl who phones her mother
a little less, then not at all. Belongingness
migrates down the spine with no one
to mind it, no one to decide whether tenderness
is worth the fuss. For too long I've been
headless, shame lugged behind me
in my tightly capped skull. I'm not looking
for praise, rather for some glossy truth
spun from my bones into lullaby. With pressure
& warm water, a lid loosens & fire grows
more precise with its flames. Imagine the burnt
leaves, the heaving soil. Imagine holding
the old ball & chain up to your ear
alone in the fields. Unleashed, I am the sound
it makes when it echoes.

Notes

The opening epigraphs are from Emily Dickinson's 1855 letter to her friend, Elizabeth Holland, and Ursula K. Le Guin's poem "The Vigil for Ben Linder" in *Going Out With Peacocks and Other Poems*.

"When a Man Cries, We Make Light of Our Own Laughter" and "Inheritances of a Twilighted Hour" reference the film, *The Sound of Music*.

"Maternal Caress, 1896" is after Mary Cassatt's painting of the same name.

"Holding My Skeleton to the Light" is inspired by Bhanu Kapil's *The Vertical Interrogation of Strangers*.

"On Sundays, I Do Laundry" references Miranda July's short story, "Roy Spivey," originally published in *The New Yorker* (June 2007).

Acknowledgments

Deepest gratitude is owed to the editors of the publications in which these poems first appeared, at times in altered versions:

The Arkansas International	"Strawberry Season"
Bayou Magazine	"Self-Portrait with Fiction & Oversized Eye"
The Burning Hearth	"I Don't Want to Write about Flowers"
Cider Press Review	"Government"
Cherry Tree	"When a Man Cries, We Make Light of Our Own Laughter"
Cream City Review	"At First, Obedience, Subsequently—"
Diode Poetry Journal	"A Room for Future Recognition"
Eastern Iowa Review	"Knitted Wings"
Gone Lawn	"Heirloom, Atmosphere, Lilies" (originally titled as "I Owe a Lot to Those I Do Not Love")
The Hunger	"I, the Unruliest Flower, Buried Winter"
The Ilanot Review	"Poem in which God or I Go Missing" ***Nominated for the Orison** *Best Spiritual Literature* **Anthology**
The Inflectionist Review	"A Student Says 'Empathy Doesn't Make Sense'" ***Nominated for the** *Best of the Net* **Anthology** "Daytime Manifesto" "Pseudo Myth"
the lickety~split	"Subject(ivity)"

Louisiana Literature	"We Examined Survival under a Microscope" "The World Ends When We Do"
The MacGuffin	"Now That My Mother Has Apologized"
Maudlin House	"Existential Poem on a Monday" "The Kids These Days Want to Be Happy"
Midway Journal	"Girl House with Epigenetic Effect, or, A Tumult of Flowers" ***Nominated for the Pushcart Prize**
On The Seawall	"River Bride"
Outskirts Literary	"Photograph Theory"
Postcard	"Idle"
San Pedro River Review	"Contemplating the Wrong Miracles"
Shō Poetry Journal	"Snow, Almost, Nearly" "Uprooted"
The Shore	"On Sundays, I Do Laundry"
Slipstream	"There Are No Warning Signs"
Smartish Pace	"In Lieu of Flowers, More Flowers" ***Finalist for the Beullah Rose Poetry Prize**
South Dakota Review	"Holding My Skeleton to the Light"
South Florida Poetry Journal	"The Language of Women"
Stirring: A Literary Collection	"Because My Tongue Is Not Welcome Here"

Sweet: A Literary Confection   "Entertainer of the Year"
"Dramatic Irony"
*Editor's Choice for the 2024 *Sweet Literary* Poetry Contest

The Tusculum Review   "Encore to Girlmaking"

"Because My Tongue Is Not Welcome Here," "On Sundays, I Do Laundry," and "Snow, Almost, Nearly" were featured on *Verse Daily*.

"Strawberry Season" was translated into Italian by Matteo Fais for *Detonatore Magazine*.

"Girl House with Epigenetic Effect, or, A Tumult of Flowers" was included in *Final Girl: An Anthology of Survival* (Porkbelly Press).

Some of these poems first appeared in the chapbook, *A Buffet Table Fit for Queens* (Washburn Prize, Small Harbor Publishing).

Gratitude

None of this would be possible without the love and support of my husband, Sean; my parents, Karyl and Michael; and my brother, Brian.

Immense gratitude to Kris Bigalk, Natasha Kane, Joel W. Coggins, and the entire Trio House Press team for making this book a reality.

Sincere appreciation to Allison Adair, Kathryn Bratt-Pfotenhauer, and Cynthia Marie Hoffman for lending their words of support.

To Helen Stonkas and Louise Leary, thank you for being a part of me.

And to every woman who has come before me and who will come after me, thank you.

About the Author

Susan L. Leary is the author of four previous poetry collections: *Dressing the Bear* (Trio House Press, 2024), selected by Kimberly Blaeser to win the 2023 Louise Bogan Award; *A Buffet Table Fit for Queens* (Small Harbor Publishing, 2023), winner of the Washburn Prize; *Contraband Paradise* (Main Street Rag, 2021); and *This Girl, Your Disciple* (Finishing Line Press, 2019), finalist for The Heartland Review Press Chapbook Prize and semi-finalist for the Elyse Wolf Prize. Her poetry and nonfiction have appeared in such places as *Indiana Review*, *Diode Poetry Journal*, *Cream City Review*, *Smartish Pace*, *The Arkansas International*, *Harpur Palate*, *Tahoma Literary Review*, and *Verse Daily*. She holds an MFA from the University of Miami and lives in Indianapolis, IN. Visit her at www.susanlleary.com.

About the Book

More Flowers was designed at Trio House Press through the collaboration of:

Kris Bigalk, Lead Editor
Natasha Kane, Interior Designer
Joel W. Coggins, Cover Designer
Yuliya Derbisheva, Cover Artist

The text is set in Adobe Caslon Pro.

About the Press

Trio House Press is an independent nonprofit press based in Minneapolis, Minnesota. We publish poetry and prose that moves, inspires, and encourages connection, empathy, and understanding, with a special emphasis on underrepresented voices and topics. To find out more about Trio House Press, please visit our website at http://www.triohousepress.org.

www.ingramcontent.com/pod-product-compliance
Lightning Source LLC
Chambersburg PA
CBHW060537080526
44586CB00012B/767